48 K

By King Jon

Introduction:

This Book is to give the true 48 Laws that bring the true Power of God.

This book is to bring an righteous understanding of power. You do not

have to manipulate, and seduce people to become successful, and powerful.

This books gives you 48 keys that will help you understand how to be a

Kingdom Citizen. The Kingdom of God is Here.

Table of Contents:

Key #/Key Title

Key 1: Always Give Glory to God

Always acknowledge God for the power you exhibit. Do not take credit for

things that wouldn't be possible without the power of God. Stay clear of

those who refuse to acknowledge the power Of God, because they hate God, and have no love in them. They will try to destroy you, so stand your

ground and praise God.

A lot of Great Writers and Artist have done some great work that makes so

much sense, but because they did not give the credit to God, and be honest

on how they was able to be introduced to every concept that led to that

work. It caused them to not prosper as well as they could have, it never

lasted. It was all do to the glory of God. This is all God's work. Never dem

your light amongst darkness.

People Like Denzel Washington always gives glory to God at his award

shows, and it's a wonderful thing to witness. He gives God glory for his

success. Every chance he gets.

Key 2: Only Trust God

It is easier for some to trust when they become comfortable, but that's when you should have your guard up the most. You can have faith in someone, but not trust them. Trust is measured by a person's connection to God. God is reliable, so will those who God sends be also.

People will trust God automatically without them knowing. When people feel God's presence they become comfortable, and begin to trust. You gain trust by being reliable. Anyone can be reliable, but it doesn't mean they

Love. Love is of God, so only trust those who are of God. Those who are of

God will Love.

Sometimes you meet people that hurt you because you trust them too

soon. People lay down, and have sex with people they've barely known for

a year. Some people have sex on first dates. This is why there is no excuse

for you when the bad result happens, because you know what you did

wrong. You didn't care who you let have access to your body. You didn't

trust that God would reveal everything if you gave God time, and only

have sex after you get married. This is hard, but possible.

Scarface didn't trust many, and he end up dying alone. He didn't have

God, so he had no rewards of God coming. He relied on his own power,

when that's never enough. You always need God.

Key 3: Always be Honest

When you walk with God you can be open about your life. Many people are not able to be open with their life because they do not walk with God.

When you walk with God nobody can stop you. You are walking in purpose. Romans 8:28 let's us know that when we Love God and walk according to our purpose it will all work out for us!

When you lie: things might go ok for a moment, but the result will show up down the line. Rather it's small or not, you will always get a reaction with any lie. If you know you want to do better: acknowledge what you did wrong so you don't risk it coming back on you in the future.

You have celebrities Like Bill Cosby, and R Kelly that many people love, that went to jail for things they did years ago. If they would have repented then, and asked for forgiveness from those they hurt, things would have

been different.

Eminem on 8 mile went up against Papa Doc, and exposed himself by

telling the truth about himself. He said everything his opponent could

possibly say against him. He exposed himself. He let everyone know he was

not hiding who he is, and went on to expose his opponent, and how he was

hiding the truth about who he was. Like how his name was Clearance, and

how his parents had a really good marriage. Also how he went to a private

school. The truth is Papa Doc was hiding living a lifestyle most people

would love to experience. He was trying to fit in.

Key 4: Speak Only The Word Of God

When you speak only the word of God you can speak as much as you want,

and power will be shown. People will gravitate toward you, but evil people

will hate you. Beware of those evil people who hate truth. To speak truth

at all times, you must never speak on anything you do not know,

comprehend, or understand completely. This helps you avoid being wrong.

The Holy Spirit spoke about in John 14:26 tells us that we will be taught

what we need to say.

Jesus always walked around speaking in parables, so only those who

needed could understand. Jesus was challenged by many people like in

Mathew 22:25 when the lawyer asked Jesus in a contentious manner

"master! What is the greatest commandment in the law"; Jesus answered

him, and told him Love God, and Love they neighbor as thy self was the

greatest commandments, upon these two commandments hang all the law.

If you stand on that and live by that, and speak that you will win.

Key 5: Nature, Character, and Authority

Your name is your nature, character, and authority. When you walk with God people will try very hard to destroy your name. You must stand firm, and always carry yourself with the nature, character, and authority of God, so your actions be your evidence. Don't worry about what people say as long as you Love God, and treat others as yourself. Don't do others the way they do you, always do what's righteous. It will all work out when you use this key and Key 3 together.

LeBron James didn't become king James just because he said he was a king. He was crowned that by his stats. His works showed who he was, and is. Having 4 championship rings and being number 1 in all time stats, his name speaks for himself, king James. Earn your name by walking like, and talking like the King God made you to be, and it will be noticed by who needs to notice.

Key 6: Always Shine In Dark Places

Make sure you speak up when you have truth in situations that could help

others. Make sure your truth is helpful not hurtful. Bringing more pain on

something broken only makes it worse. Make sure you bring love in your

words when you speak truth amongst those who need it. Stand out and

speak the word of God.

People like Yé are needed, because when he spoke out against the "Jews"(

The true chosen people of God are those who Love 1 John 4:7) Yé changed

the dynamic on how we see control. He was stripped of everything, because

of what he said. This goes against the constitution, but we didn't say

anything and everyone let it happen without speaking up for freedom of speech. This world is full of darkness, and we must be the light to shine on

the lies, and bring truth.

Key 7: Build a Kingdom

Always use your ability to bring people together to form government that can help build them using the foundation of God. A church is an example of this. Always use the people that God gives you to your advantage in righteousness. People truly want to be used, but only in a righteous manner. Give them that feeling of purpose by serving God and giving them a position in your service. Find a way that you all can serve God together. If you help others they will help you. Only help those you have around you. Only have those who love around you.

Dr. Myles Monroe is the best example of kingdom building. His motto is "changing followers into leaders, and leaders into agents of change". This is beautiful, because he did it up until he died with his wife in 2014, which he predicted he would die with his wife. He lead the Bahamas to one of the

greatest governments, and influenced many nations around him. He was

on his way to a Global Leadership Forum that was going to change the

entire world, and open up many doors. There was investigation done, but

not much information given. Become a agent of Change.

Key 8: Becoming a fisherman

Understand what people like. Learning to gain people's attention is based

on recognizing the things we all have in common. God has given us a

common understanding of Love. Go into places that others in your position

don't bother. Make sure when you do, you come with understanding of

what makes them interested in anything. Find their bait of choice, and put

in on your hook, and throw out the line with love and good fruit. When

you finish you will find a very great catch.

I will never forget when I was downtown Detroit. I was selling my Music

on Cd, and I ran into a large group of foreigners. I immediately went up to

them and started talking. Once I got their attention I rapped, and I sold a

lot of CDs, and gained great connection, and people who wanted to do work for me. Go where the crowd is, and stand out with something that will

draw them in.

Key 9: Do not Debate fools

If you are noticing a person lacks knowledge do not engage with them. It

will only make you feel and look bad in the end. Always bring correction

once and don't repeat yourself. Always leave after recognizing you are amongst swine. Mathew 7:6 let's us know to be very cautious on who we

entertain when it comes to revealing the secrets of God spoke of in proverbs

25:2.

Some celebrities stay quiet on certain topics, and are called sellouts. The

are called this because you should always speak your mind, but there is

also a understanding that even when you say what the truth is, some

people won't want to hear it, and that's the world we're living in.

Nevertheless speak up!

Key 10: Loyalty

Loyalty is being able to understand that evil can attack a person and they

can go down a dark road that only true love can bring them out of. True

Love is God. You embody God when you are loyal to those who God

Loves. God loves All who Loves. If you notice a person who has a great

heart Is struggling, and you turn your back in them to save your own life

the same will be repaid to you. Do not become involved with anyone you can't be loyal to. Only a person who Loves can be strong enough to help a

damaged person.

Forest Gump was a true example of loyalty. He only had eyes for one

woman his whole life. Even when she was lost he stayed available. Each

time she left, because of her trauma, and satanic ways he stood strong, and

took her back until eventually they started a family together. What's sad

is she still had to pay for what she did, and ended up with a virus(maybe

HIV we never found out) but you can't just give yourself away to a bunch

of people, and think you don't have to pay for it at some point. Repent

before it's too late. God gives grace, but for only so long.

Key 11: Leader Making

Being able to create leaders is the Goal of a righteous King. Having people

who are self governed is a beautiful thing. Weak Kings need full control

over their subjects which is why most kingdoms fall. God's kingdom

doesn't fall, because God wants us all to be Kings and priest(Exodus

19:6). Learn to be a true leader by being able to create leaders. The leaders

you create must follow God, there will be success even when you leave.

Big Meech was a kingpin who made a army of people who was able to come together, and become the biggest drug organization to ever exist. They lasted so long because of the leadership. Big Meech taught each member how to be their own boss. He gave them all the ability to eat just as good as him. While giving them the opportunity, he still was able to show why he was the true agent of change. His downfall was the ones who never became leaders. They didn't move like leaders they actually was dependent on him, and end up being a liability to the rest of the bosses on the team.

The reason that this is important, even though I don't condone drug dealing is the actual reason he was successful. He was successful, because he had love amongst all the members. Everything runs smoother when everyone is on the same level. Don't keep others dependent on you, unless

you want them to become a liability in the long run. Instead show them

how to create the same energy you do, so when you not around they can

have the same energy present.

Key 12: Beware of Witchcraft

Learning that manipulation for evil is witchcraft. To manipulate a person

isn't wrong, but to manipulate with unrighteous intent is witchcraft. When

your actions hurt someone it's unrighteous. Be careful. Witchcraft is also

using the omen and warning of God given to us in Genesis 1:14 to

manipulate people to believe things are out of God's control. This is all

witchcraft to take the laws of God, and use it for unrighteousness. Always

be honest when you know it can help. Beware of people who withhold

information that can help you. They don't love you.

Lord Voldemort was stopped because of the love of Harry Potter's mother.

His spell was broken, and he was sent away. No matter how much a person makes you believe they are powerful, always remember they are nothing

without Love. Love is the law God set in place to conquer all.

Key 13: Always Offer something

Find a way to offer something to the world. When you have something to

exchange you will always have what you need. When you offer someone

something they need they will always be more willing to help you with what you need. Use your gifts to create something that's valuable to others.

I remember I gave my 6th grade crush some candy and she liked me every since that day. I also remember I bought this one girl some AirPods Pros, and she gave me whatever I wanted after that, without me giving much more. Basically I gave a little, and I gained a lot. The thing is my intentions were never to gain anything, but the satisfaction of my partner.

I also wrote 7 books, which now gives me passive income. I put in some work for a certain amount of time, and gained a eternal source of income, and the same with my music, clothing, and Videos, so now I have many things to offer in exchange for other resources.

Key 14: Love Your Enemy

Learning to love your enemy requires your to understand them. They can

not hurt you when you are coming from a place ahead of where they are

going. Learn them and love them and you will change them. You must

have love in you to accomplish this. Love is hard when you don't know

what it is. Practice love. Love is: patience, understanding, care, correction,

long suffering, loyalty, and faithfulness simultaneously.

In a show called Dragon ball super there is a man named Goku, who has a

enemy named vegeta who becomes his friend. He also has an enemy named

Frieza who tried to kill him. Goku defeated Frieza, but gave him many

chances. One day there was a tournament that would destroy the whole

universe they were from, and Goku needed Frieza to help on behalf of their

universe against other universes. Frieza ended up helping Goku when he

was almost defeated, and that resulted in them winning the tournament.

Your enemies might become a help to you at some point, if you always

show love and mercy.

Key 15: The Art Of Healing

Learning to heal instead of destroying is a powerful key. This Key is about

learning how to give to a person what they need to help them see where

they are wrong without offending them. This allows them to see the space

for change and the clear need to change. Some people aren't able to heal,

because of their own self. Others can heal if you love them instead of hurt, and destroy them completely. People can take advantage of you helping

them heal. You have to be a powerful person to do this. When you are

weak, that person can seek to destroy you for correcting them.

When Malcom X went to prison he was able to heal. He was surrounded by

positive influence. He was taken away from the world, and isolated, so he

can heal and learn who he was. He had to transform his mind. Even

though he didn't master what Love is, he embodied it the best he could and

he helped others heal as well. While becoming one of the biggest influences

in history he was hated by his own people, and the government, leaving his

untimely murder up for debate to some.

Key 16: Value Your Time

Always be strategic when giving your presence, energy, or words. Limit

access, but never to those who need it. Always be aware of those who need

you even while avoiding those who don't.

I know I sound like a kid referencing cartoons like Dragon ball z, but when

I was a kid I wanted for so long for another episode, and about 20 years

later a new season premiered, and the value was so much higher, due to the

fact I could have died before that season premiered. I lost my little brother

before it premiered. I could no longer watch it with him. He couldn't enjoy

it like I could. When you don't have access to something it helps you

appreciate it so much more. The memories that were brought back had an

effect of its own.

Key 17: Be not of this world

When you become like God, you become everything satan is not. This

makes you different, and people love different. Be like God in every way,

and you will shine bright everywhere there is darkness. Make sure you

understand that God is spontaneous, not predictable.

J. Cole is a great artist who doesn't conform to the fancy lifestyle. He is a

humble artist, who likes to be low key. Because he speaks a positive

message he doesn't get as much play on the radio, but his numbers still

I know I sound like a kid referencing cartoons like Dragon ball z, but when

I was a kid I wanted for so long for another episode, and about 20 years

later a new season premiered, and the value was so much higher, due to the

fact I could have died before that season premiered. I lost my little brother

before it premiered. I could no longer watch it with him. He couldn't enjoy

it like I could. When you don't have access to something it helps you

appreciate it so much more. The memories that were brought back had an

effect of its own.

Key 17: Be not of this world

When you become like God, you become everything satan is not. This

makes you different, and people love different. Be like God in every way,

and you will shine bright everywhere there is darkness. Make sure you

understand that God is spontaneous, not predictable.

J. Cole is a great artist who doesn't conform to the fancy lifestyle. He is a

humble artist, who likes to be low key. Because he speaks a positive

message he doesn't get as much play on the radio, but his numbers still shine through, because he is a blessing. He produces good fruit. He has not

switched up yet, and he continues to become more known. Do not be like

everyone else because it's popular or will get your views, or plays.

Key 18: Armor Of God

This Key is about learning That God is Love and Love is the Armor of

God. Practice Love, and you will be protected. Do not act like you want to love when you don't, because your heart doesn't lie. You can't gain

protection until you acknowledge you don't have it.

Every successful person has to realize life isn't about them. Life is about

others. Learning to making other happy is the key to life. Serving others

create opportunities to ask for help. We all need help. Make sure your goal

is helping others, so the help you receive will always be beneficial to more

than just yourself.

Key 19: Know Your Enemies

Do not think when you walk the path to the kingdom of God that you

won't have people who will want to kill you. They don't matter. Their

feelings only matter when you focus on them, and not God. Know as much

as you can about all those who hate you, but understand if you know satan

then you know all of them. Stay alert. Lions get attacked, but it's the

outcome that shows the name.

People spent so much time hating during the presidential term of Donald

Trump, that they didn't notice how he helped create a more independent

thought process in America. He did in my opinion do a better job that

George W. Bush, His father, Ronald Reagan, and many other presidents,

yet he was disrespected by the media and lied on. His words were taking out of context, and he was mocked by his own country to other countries.

Through all of this he recognized what they were doing, called it out, and

finished strong.

Key 20: Commit to God

There is a universal understanding of what is right. Rape, theft, murder,

abuse, and betrayal. These things hurt and we know they are wrong. God created a law against these things. Learning God's law will help you not

hurt. Follow God. Learning the word of God by studying the Bible, and

every ancient text that gives experience. 2 Timothy 3:16 says that all

writings are inspired by God, and should be used for doctrine, reproof,

correction, and instruction in a righteous manner. Trust what God says is

Right. People you come in contact with, must be committing to God before

you decide to allow them in your life. If they submit to God you can

submit to them. Learning who God is will be the first step. God is the

balanced masculine and feminine force of all things that exist.

Nick Cannon had a podcast where he had a guest that he was speaking

with, things were said like white people were from the caucasus mountains, and they lose their thyroid gland, which causes them to be more aggressive.

These statements got him fired from his show, and taking off air. He

apologized, and he got his show back. He didn't know his enemy, and paid

the cost.

Key 21: Understanding

Understanding allows you to understand how people think and behave. You can understand that you can make a person feel special by listening to them. Making them feel heard. Use this to your advantage to help them understand God's love through you, even when they might be wrong. Understanding what makes them think the way they do by asking them questions. People love to answer questions they have the answer to.

Schools created something called special Ed. They claim it's for kids who need more attention. The truth is, some kids don't all learn the same way. You can say something, but that doesn't mean that it would be understood the same way by everyone. The best thing a teacher can do is ask does anyone have questions, and take time to answer the questions from those who don't understand, so you can better understand their

misunderstanding. With this method there would be no need to single kids

out, and claim they have learning disabilities. Try to understand the

method each kid learns and take time out. It's always more people who feel

the same way, but they may be less vocal which will make it seem nobody

else feels the same way or have the same questions.

Key 22: Getting Back Up

Proverbs 24:16 tells us that a wise man falls 7 times and gets back up, but

the wicked will fall into mischief. When you fall take time to heal and

recover. Study where you can improve, and try again. Defeat is an

experience that creates redemption. Redemption exist so you can

understand how it feels to be someone in a low place, but you can also show

how that doesn't have to be the end. Your defeat is an set up for a future win, that win means so much more than the defeat, that allows you to have

that much better victory speech.

Rocky Balboa lost against Mr T, but he went and figured out what he had

to do different. He worked harder. He trained diligently. He then won and

beat Mr T. When The Russian killed Apollo Creed, and Rocky watch the

fight, and was destroyed in the inside, from losing his friend. Rocky fell

down, and knew he couldn't lose when the time came. He trained hard, and

beat the Russian everyone thought was unstoppable. Over come the fall

and get back up, and go harder.

Key 23: Productivity of the Mind

Find a way to use your mind to create, and be productive. You can always

find something to create. Rather it's a book, a picture, a food, business, a

song, or a video. We have the ability to be productive. Use your mind to

create fresh ideas. Always use your time to be productive to stop from

making unproductive decisions. Find people that are able to connect the

product you create.

Eddie Murphy played in a Movie called Dolamite, and it was about a man

who wanted to become famous. Dolamite would do live performances of standup comedy, make comedy records that created passive income. He

eventually started to want more. He continued to create rather he knew if

he would have an audience or not. His consistent creating landed him a lot

of attention. As he gained the attention he didn't stop there. He wrote a

screen play, and got people to help bring it to life. The movie became so big

Eddie Murphy got to play the role of the legend in a modern day

reenactment of the movie. This also motived me to write Mind Made

Volume 1 & 2, which are seasons to my own personal television series. Stay

creating until you are empty of ideas. Don't make the graveyard rich.

Key 24: Become Meek

Once you know who God is you, and you follow God everything will make

more sense. Do not worry about who is stronger than you. Respect people

in higher positions. Only allow people who can recognize person over

position, get the privilege of getting to close to you. It will make it easy for

you not to have expectations on how you must move to get into places,

that you must demonstrate the work of God. Recognizing moving in the world versus being of the world is different. Learn to move in the world while not being of the world. We are nothing without God

DC Young Fly is a young comedian that started off making videos talking trash about celebrities. While he did this he never cared, or considered what level the people he was speaking on were on. He stayed consistent with key 23 and he got a response from Kevin hart, and a few other celebrities that brung him up to the level they were at by just responding. Position is an illusion. You are as powerful as you understand you are. DC Young Fly has now become the biggest Wild n Out star, and an actor, along with being the third member of a 3 man team podcast called 85 south.

Key 25: Become Like Christ

You must understand what Love is. You must change your way of

thinking from how the world wants you to think. Learn How to speak with

the word of God. You have to come in the name Of God. Love is that

name. Learning to love like Christ is the Goal of Life. That is the

kingdom. You have to become one with Christ. You have to be with

Christ. You have to be Christ. To be Christ you have to call of the name of

God. By walking in Love.

Martin Luther King Jr did his best to walk, and talk like Christ, and he

loved a nation. He did have human qualities that caused him to be

stopped. Every piece of corrupt energy is a danger to your success.

Years after he died a movie called Selma depicted him smoking cigarettes,

and having a potential affair on his wife. These things could have be a

causes to why it was easy to take him out like they did. When you have

habits, you must get rid of them as fast as possible, before they be a burden

in your future. We all do wrong, but it's the ability to grown, and learn while being an example on being better. Don't hide your flaws but repent

like Jesus said.

Key 26: Become perfect

Mathew 5:48 tells us to be perfect Like God, and the way to do that is by

practicing being, patient, caring, understanding, corrective, long suffering,

faithful, and loyal simultaneously. These 7 actions make up the balance of

God. The balance of God is Love. When you mess up make sure you repent.

Recognizing why what you did was not the best method, is key to future

success. Trying to find ways to make wrong right takes away the ability to

think of new successful outcomes.

We have a misunderstanding of what perfect is. The Bible tells us that

Noah was perfect in his generation(Genesis 6:9) but he got drunk in his

vineyard and passed out naked for his son Ham to see. This by modern day

definition isn't "perfect". What perfect truly is, is being able to learn from

your wrongs, and do the best you can to avoid evil. You must practice this

and make it a habit to be considered perfect. Being perfect doesn't mean

you won't do things wrong. It means you will always eventually get

everything right.

Key 27: understanding Bread of Life

People have a need for God, rather they like it or not. If you fill people

with the information that brings them closer to the power of God, they will

seek you out. Do not let anyone give you God's glory. Always be humble,

and lead your followers to God's Kingdom. Make sure the words you speak

always edify, and heal those who hear. Fill yourself with the words of

Christ, and regurgitate what Jesus said like you do your music favorite artist. Mathew 6:22 tells us to fill our minds with only light. When you become this light, and gain following, give your followers righteous tasks to complete to help them feel fulfilled.

Pastor Solomon Kinloch Jr, is a pastor of Triumph Church. Triumph is one of the fastest growing churches in America. Pastor Kinloch started at the church in his early 20's. The church had only one building, but when he came bringing the word of God every Sunday, word got out, and the church got pack on Liddesdale and Omaha in southwest Detroit. He kept pouring the word so much and feeding so many, his church grew into 5 different locations, and buildings. He now has a new location in

Philadelphia as well, after helping a struggling church. When you give the

bread of life, the children of God will definitely help you build what is

necessary to give the bread to even more people. Feed your sheep.

Key 28: Fear God

When you fear God it will become the beginning of wisdom; proverbs 9:10

tells us this.

When you trust in God you should put aside all other fears. Be able to

stand strong behind the word of God, and you will always succeed. The

Holy Spirit will come to you at your time of need to deliver you if you keep

your faith and only fear God

Mike Tyson was one of the greatest boxers to ever live. He lived a very

sinful life while he was becoming a great fighter. He was betrayed by

many, he was set up many times, and he was lied on by many women. As

he learned that his success wasn't his it was from God, he humbled himself.

He now uses every moment to teach us all that God is the reason. Love is

the action to follow. If he had a chance he would go back, and include God

in every decision he made. I thank mike Tyson for becoming the man he is

today before he dies. He is currently 56, and he goes on many podcasts, and

speak his positive message, and amazing testimony.

Key 29: God's Vision for man

When you diligently seek God you will receive a exclusive vision. This

vision must be planned out once received. Make sure you detail every part

of this vision in word form. Write or type out this entire vision along with

the type of people you will, and won't allow close to your vision. Your

vision will never come from God and not be clear. Unclear vision causes

confusion for you.

Nepoleon Hill once said that he didn't know what to call his book "Think and Grow Rich". When he came up with the name he had it come to him after contemplating on many other names. He had to write the book down first and make it clear, so he could then truly think of a great name. If the book, or vision of the book wasn't written he would have never come up with the name for his book. The vision comes before the title. The head of every woman is the man and the head of every man is Christ. Christ rings the vision!

Key 30: Life is a Weight

Thank God for grace, so that you can learn, and grow from your experience

to become stronger. Life doesn't get easier, but you get stronger. Life is a

weight, that weighs 1,000lbs. It won't ever get lighter, but you can become

stronger by not giving up, and learning from every mistake. The stronger

you get the easier it feels and looks. As you get stronger recognizing that it's still weaker people in the world who might need your help. Do not

make them feel less then, but give them understanding of why it's easier

for you.

When I was 19 I got my first car, and I got pulled over for so many

different things. I had many tickets pile up. I started to miss court, and get

pulled over, and get arrested for bench warrants. As I got older I started to

notice why this was happening. I wasn't following the law of the land. I

wasn't being fully obedient to the laws. The Bible tells us in Romans 13:1-7

that we should always do what is good. It is always good to follow law.

When we find the law we tell others they can as well, and that creates

chaos. Once I adjusted, and moved with caution my tickets cut down significantly. I thank God I have avoided many tickets since, and even had

times where I was pulled over, and because I was meek, I was given grace,

and no ticket. Always do what is lawful, and things will become easier.

Practice making following the law a habit, and life will become easier.

Key 31: Set the Tone

Always use the power that God has given you to create a need for what you

have. By discovering God's secrets you become valuable. Use this value to draw in people, and show them what nobody else has been able to. Use the

Unique Gifts God has given you to control the energy that needs to be felt

in any atmosphere. Start off by making a factual statement that is

controversial. This will make you the center of attention. When no one can

prove you wrong, and they come with their feelings you will appear more

credible.

Brother Polight is a conscious community leader, and leader of the new

black panther movement, who has many controversial things surrounding

him. He made a scene by quoting Dr York saying "the black woman is

god". Psalms 82:6 tells us we are all gods children of the most high, so his

statement wasn't wrong. It was a strong controversial statement. This gave him attention where he was then able to produce the other knowledge

he was introduced to the world that has helped us grow in consciousness as

a whole. Find a way to make them notice you have something to say.

Key 32: Being Optimistic

Being able to look at things in a good way is a key from God. You must be

able to get others to see the good parts of all things. There is Good in

everything. Find a way to communicate harsh reality in a pleasant

manner. Try to create the image of peace while presenting the reality of

discomfort. Nothing last forever except what's with God, so anything bad

isn't permanent.

Rather we Like it or not be the artist formerly known as Kanye West is a

master of optimism. He has always seen the good in everything he had

going on. He seen the opportunity Sway didn't see when he told Ye' that

he should do things a different way. Ye' was able to succeed, because he

seen the good in the situation he took part in. He was able to reach billionaire status while everyone else was trying to make him look at the

bad in his strategy. He continued to look at the good even now after he lost

all of his endorsements with the Jewish community, for practicing freedom

of speech.

Key 33: Everyone is Human

Some people become weak because they can't see the weakness of others.

Some people are physically strong, but at the same time emotionally weak.

Some people are beautiful, but insecure. Some people are rich, but have no discipline. Understanding others weakness helps you recognize your own strengths. You have weakness, but you have strength. Don't allow another to down play your strength, because of your weakness. Being able to show someone their weakness will humble them. Do not use others weakness to hurt them, but instead help them.

Kimbo Slice was a street boxer that was very tough. He was very muscular, and big. He knocked one of his opponents eye out. He was undefeated until he switch lanes. He eventually began to fight in the UFC platform. He won his first match, but was worn out by his opponent Huston Alexander who was able to kick Kimbo and put him down. Huston could have finished Kimbo, but he allowed Kimbo time to get up.

Nevertheless Kimbo eventually even though he was the greatest street

fighter we had known, he was knocked out in 14 seconds by UFC fighter

Seth Petruzelli. This was a clear indication that no matter how big or

strong a person seems to be, they have their weaknesses.

Key 34: Know Who You Are

When you come in God's name don't allow those less than you grab your attention. Do not address things that have no intelligence. God doesn't argue. To be like God, you must act like God. The sons of God John 1:12 carry themselves differently than the majority. Have purpose behind all that you speak and do. Hold yourself to a high standard and firm integrity. Tupac Shakur was a legend. He was a young preforming arts student, that eventually went on to create his image. He believed, and had faith that he was a thug. He carried his self in that complete image, and knew who he was. This confidence in who he was, became attractive to the masses, and

he went on to be part of the Hip Hop Hall Of Fame. If he would have knew he was anointed, and walked in the name of God with that same faith, he would have been protected from harms way. Him knowing who he was,

gave him the power, but him not knowing who's he was cost him the

power.

Key 35: Patience of God

Be able to recognize discomfort inside yourself before you act on any situation. Analyze every outcome before acting. Be able to let a person fully finish before speaking. Allow other impatient people to go before you. Recognizing the impatience of others helps see your own. If something isn't happening, and you doing everything to make it happen, then you must wait. Do not stop doing what you should though, or it will never happen.

James 5:7-11 tells you how Job from the Bible was patient even through the trials and tribulations. Even in Job 2:9 when his wife said to him "curse God, and die". He told her she sounded foolish, and he said "should we accept the good that God has given, but not the bad"? He kept his faith.

Steve Harvey was once homeless living out his car. He spent his time doing

stand up. He didn't not get paid much, but he followed Key 23 & 24 and

one day he got a call that put him in position to perform in front of people

who would eventually get him his own show and much more. Never think

your position is permanent. Just make sure you appreciate your position

while you have it. Be the best at your position. A master fry cook, is

greater than a incompetent CEO.

Key 36: Wanting What's for You

When you walk with God you must not want things that are not good for you. Whenever you don't have something, it's because it's not good for you at that time. Focus on what makes you want whatever it is in the first place. Most times you won't have a logical reason on wanting things you can't have except it looks good, or sounds nice. You must know that what's for you will come to you. When you want things that are not good for you, it can destroy you if you acquire it. Anytime you have to go against God to acquire something it's not from God. Seek the Kingdom and

All the things you desire will come(Mathew6:33)

Dave Chappelle is a perfect example of not wanting what is not good for

you. Dave turned down 50 million dollars, because he refused to throw

away his integrity. He was outcast in Hollywood, and couldn't get work,

until he left , and came back to make a 50 million dollar deal with Netflix

for 2 of his shows. He blew up, and became the biggest comedian in

history. He is also one of my personal favorite comedians. He denied the

gifts from Satan and received the gifts from God. Everything that looks

good doesn't lead to good things.

Key 37: Creating Attention

Learn what attracts the world by studying what's popular, and use these

things to introduce your message. Use your voice, clothes, and other

worldly resources to grab attention with righteous intentions.

Manipulation is powerful when used for good. Most people only move when

others do. Learn to move people by moving others.

Lecrae is a Grammy winning Hip Hop artist who raps for God. He found a

way to make creating music for God so popular he actually won a

Grammy, and was number one on iTunes multiple times, speaking nothing

but the word of God. He used this key with perfection. Going on to start

his own record label, also using Key 7 to his advantage building a kingdom.

Key 38: Being a friend to Satan

Satan isn't immune to being manipulated. Be a good friend to Satan even when Satan acts evil towards you. Learn to recognize when Satan is trying to provoke you, and avoid anger, but instead show love. This will cause Satan to look bad, and Satan hates to look bad. Satan will then try to play nice for the remainder of the situation. Satan will use your connection to God to make others think you are speaking down on them. Knowledge should never be hated. When you notice a hate towards knowledge start to realize it's time to manipulate Satan into thinking you are his friend. You are his friend, just not for the purpose he wants, but for the purpose of defending God's name. Don't care about the criticism you will receive, just

hold your ground it earns more respect.

I remember watching a documentary on Kobe Bryant. Kobe was a star,

and was really the leader of his team, and one of the leader of the entire

NBA. Kobe wanted to win games, but he wanted his teammates to also

work just as hard as him, but their laziness caused them to slack. Kobe did

something that is important. He used this key number 38, and pretended

to be friends, and go out with his teammates.

The next morning as they were coming in Kobe was dressed ready to head

to the gym and work out, and told them since he hung out with them they should hang out with him, and he started a trend with his teammates

fighting against the satanic laziness that was over them.

Key 39: Being in control

Control a conversation by making strong statements that causes the other to be off balance while also keeping your own balance. Do not let yourself get angry, or you will expose your lack of love. Always come in love. Love makes Satan uncomfortable.

Most people underestimate the level of control Donald Trump showed during his presidential debates against Joe Biden in 2020. Trump spoke on all the things that Joe Biden did that was a sign of his lack of love. As Trump called himself the greatest president since Abraham Lincoln, Joe Biden became uncomfortable, because Trump was known to be somewhat corrupt, so he was able to stand his ground while Joe Biden, wasn't use to being seen in the light.

He was able to control the debate by pointing out the Lack of Love of Joe

Biden while staying Calm on his turns. The key was that he addressed

things that made Joe Biden uncomfortable to speak on causing an

unbalance in his responses, feeling the need to defend himself.

Key 40: Always appreciate Gifts

Stay away from anyone who gives you something, and then asked you

from anything. Always have intentions to help those who need it though.

If you can help a person always help them. Do not measure what you give

on what you get. Never measure what you get to what you will give. God

uses all to bless all. Be careful of the intentions of those who give to you,

and what you accept. Accepting things from people you know hate you,

can cause you to become cursed.

Lil Wayne is one of the greatest Hip Hop Artists of all time. Wayne was

put on by Birdman. This was a gift to Wayne. Wayne's whole career was

led by Birdman. Lil Wayne had no problem, because he felt like Birdman was doing him a favor. This Gift from Birdman came with a price that started to seem unbalanced to Wayne. Eventually, because Birdman owned all of Wayne's work things became heated when Wayne wanted to work for himself, or any other labels. At first it was a struggle for Wayne to get what was rightfully his, because it all seem like a gift from Birdman. They sorted it out, and they still have a decent relationship. Always be careful of what gifts you accept, but always appreciate what you do accept.

Key 41: Understanding your Role under God

You should never claim to fill God's shoes. You are second to God always.

Always make this clear to yourself, and those who say otherwise.

Your role is to serve God. All those who follow you must follow God first.

You are a great man under God.

There was a Kid named Bonk Gang Aka John Gabbana. Gabbana used to

go around it do wicked pranks On random people, until one of his pranks

backfired on him, because it was not of God what he was doing, and someone broke his jaw. He disappeared, and reappeared as a man who was

seeking a relationship with God. From that time forward he tried to be

positive, and spread positivity. Always understand that nothing without

God leads to prosperity in the end. Fame is temporary, but the soul is

forever.

Key 42: Beware Of satan's Presence

Make sure you lock down any satanic energy you notice before it spreads.

Manage your surroundings by making sure you don't allow anyone who

isn't submissive to the word of God around you. Separate yourself from

people who you notice doesn't love. Be able to discern what a person's

intentions are. It's not them that you have have to be stern towards, but

it's the energy working within them, Ephesians 6:12.

Fred Hampton was the Chairman of the Black Panther Movement, and he

led one of the biggest Political Parties to exist. He became a threat to the

government. He would be able to infiltrate the United Sates Government if

he got enough support. What the United States Government did allegedly,

was send in William O'Neal who copped a plea, and infiltrated the black panther party, and set Fred Hampton up to die. This was portrayed in a

movie from 2021 titled Judas The Black Messiah.

Key 43: The Moods of Man

Learning what makes people happy, sad, mad, or glad is key to being able

to tap into their mind, and guide them towards what you want. You must

love each person you use this key with. If you do not love it will play out

bad for you in the end. This key is the way to gain access to the power of

others. This is how you build a kingdom of likeminded individuals. This

key must be used with balance as if it was used with God.

Jay Z appealed to the masses by creating a Cult like movement called Roc

Nation. This movement allowed Jay to bring people in that appealed to

the masses, like Rihanna, Kanye West, and J cole all became their own

bosses. Jay Z knew how to please the people around them to help him

please the rest of the world, also marrying one of the world's favorite women Beyoncé. This combination made him twice as appealing to the

masses playing in their need to believe, that a man who isn't the most

handsome can have a woman so attractive. If Jay Z would have given God

the glory he would be more powerful than some of his partners.

Key 44: Fighting Like Satan

To defeat any enemy you must learn them. Satan has found ways to grab

the minds of the people. Use this key to use satan's methods with

righteousness, and you will always over power and succeed in any situation

were this methodology is loved. Learning to use things like music, movies,

and podcasts can be great tools to reverse the effects satan forces on

people's subconscious.

Snoop Dogg has created a movement to bring bloods and crips together.

He has a song called "One blood, One cuzz" that promotes the unity of

gangs across America. Snoop Dogg is using his gifts to do the work of God.

He also made a gospel album, That pushes positive energy. Snoop is a perfect example of Key 44. Use your influence to help the people see the

Glory of God.

Key 45: Be Human

Be able to show your human side while holding your integrity in place, and morals. Do not be embarrassed to express things that helped you become who you are. Growth is the purpose of life. Make sure you do your best to be the best version of yourself, and the rest will follow. Your past doesn't change your future; your present day actions are what does that. Give the people around you the same time to grow. Be patient while they learn and make mistakes as you have as well.

Will Smith made one of the most life changing decisions in his life at the 2022 Oscars. His first time winning an Oscar, and he was banned for slapping Chris Rock for making a joke, about his wife. He was being human. We got to see the real will smith. He was being manipulated by his wife, as well as being under peer pressure from the media surrounding his

relationship. He felt the need to defend his name. It didn't work out, but

he learned and grew from that situation. He got to be an example for

others who could be put in the same situation.

Key 46: Carry Your Cross

When you walk with God and appear to be perfect, and you yourself don't

acknowledge your perfection you will attract Satan. Do not let Satan stop

you from expressing the perfect words of God on why you believe. Do not

let the hate of others being used by satanic energy drift your point. Be

perfect in the name of God, and stand on it even if people hate it. They can

not beat God, or stop God.

Jesus was taken to the highest mountain and shown all the kingdoms(

Mathew 4:9). He could have had it all. But he chose to carry his cross and

do the will of God. Jesus didn't need the luxury type of life. He just needed

the Kingdom of God. Jesus faced his enemies daily, and greatness came everywhere he went. Jesus endured a lot of pain, but never gave up on the

will of God.

Every time that Jesus was tempted he always responded with a perfect

answer.

Key 47: When will the end Come

A lot of people don't know this key. Jesus told us when the end will come, and people still say we don't know. That's because they are not of God. The knowledge of God is only given to those who call on God's name, and diligently seek God. Mathew 24:14 tells us after the Gospel of the Government of God is preached unto the whole world to all nations then the end will come. The Kingdom is Love. We must learn what love is, and how to Love God. Once this happens we can spread it to the whole world, and then the end will come.

Our only goal is to spread love. We must learn how to Love, and we must build a political party that's built on the foundation of Christ. We must believe on the name of God. This political party will only be available to

the children of God. We will infiltrate the Government, and spread the

Gospel of the Kingdom to the United Nations, and create peace across the

world under God.

Key 48: Follow God

To truly follow God you must let go of all the worldly things, and worldly

people who have a hold on you. Learning to understand that God has given

you a way to provide without needing anyone, the name of God, which is

love. Love is the nature, character, and authority of God. We must move in

Love, and find our purpose without staying stuck where the world is

happy, but instead spreading the Kingdom of Love. 1 John 4:7 tells us God

is love so we should definitely Love to be more like God.

Learning to Love has been mentioned many times. The true Key of God is

Love. When you truly learn how to Follow God you will learn how to Love,

and this will give you access to all 48 Keys Of God.

Made in the USA
Middletown, DE
16 January 2023